7 KEYS TO MENDING A BROKEN MIND

By Patricia Evans Morrisey

Permission can be obtained by writing to:
Patricia Evans Morrisey
PO Box 923
Hamlet, NC 28345

Or via email at:
pat-evans@att.net

***

Dedicating this book to: My Lord and Savior Jesus Christ for entrusting me with this journey. My Best Friend/Soulmate/Husband, Ronnie Morrisey (aka Mr.) for your love and support, my Sons, Robert, Tony, Daron, & Antwan, all 8 of my Grand Darlings (my inspiration and joy), my parents, Sisters, friends, and all of the people that will take the journey

CONTENTS

Mending Broken Minds

INTRODUCTION:

Our expectations don't always match our experiences. When dealing with the mind, we must be very careful because it's so powerful. We can be sitting at home and think about something that happened when we were a child. We can remember the date, time, place, who was there, and even certain smells.

Not only that, our mind can learn something when we are 3, 4, or 5 and be able to recall it until we die...How many of y'all know the Alphabets? I still remember Singing- A,B,C,D,E,F,G,H, I,J,K,L (LET ME PAUSE RIGHT HERE SO YOU CAN FINISH SINGING THE SONG...LOL). So how old were you when you learned the Alphabet? How old are you now? Remember, each time you get ready to say or use them, you don't have to go back and relearn them. You automatically recall them. I told you the mind was powerful. The mind is our think center and at times we think too much about things that we cannot control. This causes us to lose focus and not think clearly. The mind was not created to worry, stress over daily life challenges or struggles, or even be anxious.

Once our thinking is unclear, we begin to say some not so Godly things, go to some not so Godly places, do crazy (whatever your crazy is) stuff, and settle for things that we wouldn't settle for under any other circumstances. Once our thinking is unclear, before we know it; our bright days become dim and our dark nights seem darker. We live behind so many masks. We have been taught and/or we learned to walk around with a smile on our faces when our mind and heart feel like it's in a zillion pieces. It appears to others that we are unstable, but many times, we don't want to accept or see (not that we can't see) what others see.

I remember trying to hold on to a man (not relationship) that wasn't good for me. To me, we were in a relationship, but to him, **he** was not. I remember making excuses for this man day after day deceiving myself and relying on my feelings and emotions to a point that my mind accepted the fact that I was in a relationship with this man.

I knew right from wrong, and I wanted to do right, but my feelings and emotions kept me stuck. I was an emotional train wreck that happened. You see, I have been the other woman. I have been the side piece. I have been the "secret" that everybody knew about but me. I have fornicated. I kept hanging around when I knew I needed to let go, but I allowed myself to be used instead of being rejected.

Rejection was my biggest fear. Where did it come from? I had to search my heart and mind to figure it out. While searching my mind, I realized that my rejection started when I was 4 years old. It didn't just happen to me when I was an adult. Rejection was rooted down inside of me and fear drove my emotions and feelings. At times, I thought I was crazy.

You see, when I was a child, you could go to school if you turned 5 anytime during that year. My birthday is in December. Somewhere between enrolling and going to kindergarten, the date changed and in order to go to school, you had to be 5 by September or October 1. I was enrolled in school only to be told that I couldn't go anymore. I wanted to go to school. I loved learning. I didn't do anything wrong, so why couldn't I go to school? Everybody else went to school.

I really didn't understand what was happening, so of course, the next morning, I got ready for school. Needless to say, I couldn't go. I remember crying all day waiting on my sisters to get home from school. I felt a feeling in my heart and way down in my stomach that I had never felt before. I felt fear of being left out, put out, and/or cast out for no good reason. The seed of rejection was planted. Some may say that's hard to believe, but I watered that seed (rejection) that latched on to me as a small child for almost 50 years. The harvest was plenteous, but not good. I had low self-esteem, I pretended to be okay, and I did a lot of things to be accepted by others.

I had to figure out why I made the decisions that I made and/or did the things I did to be accepted by others. Never realizing that I had never fully accepted myself. I always felt that I wasn't good enough. I always gave my last and did without so that I wouldn't be rejected. I wanted to feel accepted and I denied being rejected. I now realize that I was double minded. I was trying to please God and others so that I wouldn't get hurt.

James 1: 8 (KJV) says that " A double minded man (and woman) is unstable in all his ways". When I think about double minded, I think a person is "unsteady, inconsistent, and unable to decide". My biggest fear was being rejected so when I loved, I loved hard. I gave 100% of me. I look back and see how I went around the same mountain with different people and things. Affairs of the heart was my struggle. I was overweight, had 3 sons by the time I was 20 years old, and I felt that no man would every love me as I was.

Some people say that God delivered them and they changed instantly. That didn't happen to me. I was saved and I loved God. I wanted to (and still do) honor God and obey His word, but I also loved that man that I was with. My mind stayed on him. It was hard for me to go to sleep if I didn't see him that day. I had a lot to worry about because he wasn't just my man, he was somebody else's man too. It was like my mind got stuck and kept skipping a beat back to him forgetting that I wasn't the only woman. I tried to leave him, but I couldn't. It wasn't the sex. It wasn't for support. It wasn't for love. I was simply afraid to be by myself. I couldn't handle being rejected again.

All my life, I heard having a piece of man is better than not having a man at all. You have to be very careful who and what you listen to. I thought it was normal to just have a "man" in your life. To be honest, I don't ever remember anybody telling me what a relationship was supposed to be like and/or look like. I knew he was supposed to work because my daddy was a man and he worked. I knew I was supposed to be physically attracted to him because my mama used to tell my daddy she loved him, and they would joke around, hug, and he called her his "sweet thang", " honey", "sugar", and "darling". My daddy worked and paid the bills. This is what I wanted. A man that worked, paid bills, that would tell me he loved me, joke around with me, and call me sweet things like my daddy did. Oh, I forgot he had to be fine and sexy! I guess that was to validate me and/or to show others that I had a fine man.

I got just what I wanted. I realize now that the brokenness in me attracted the brokenness in men. Trying to fix them hoping they would love, respect, and be with me. I set out on a journey to love like this. My "wild" imagination was fueled by the ups and downs in the relationship. It's very important to be aware of what enters your mind and what you think on. My mind told me that having a piece of man was better than having no man at all.

I met what my heart and mind desired, but I wasn't ready for what I got in return. At first, all was well. We went to church together. This man was fine! This man worked. This man paid bills. This man protected me. He accepted my sons. But one day, the "real him" showed up. He didn't respect me. He would hang out with the "fellas". He chose crack cocaine over me and the crack won every pay day. He paid bills, (even though he took the money back and used it for drugs). He pawned our car. He verbally abused me. He rode other women around in my car. I continued to cook every day. I washed his clothes. I made sure he had what he needed and wanted. I forgave him so many times that I can't even remember what I forgave him for. He even moved in with the woman across the street from me on his birthday! Can you imagine seeing your husband living across the street, washing this lady's car, and playing outside with her son? To some I looked like a fool, but to me, having a piece of man was better than not having a man at all. To answer the question in your mind…..YES, I still loved him. I still slept with him when he came to see me (he even brought her son with him).

I look back and realize that I was determined to hold on and he was determined to see how far he could go before I let go. I knew he wasn't good for me, but something had a hold on me that was so strong that I felt that I needed this man. At that time, He was the best that I could get or my other option was to be by myself. Yes, I worried about what he was doing, where he was, and/or who he was with. Truth be told, I know where he was, what he was doing, and who he was doing it with, but my mind wouldn't accept that. A double mind is a terrible thing because even though I knew where he was, what he was doing and who he was doing it with; I could make him be (in my mind) where ever I wanted him to be. I remember convincing myself that he was too tired after working, or he probably got called in to work, and/or he had to take his mother somewhere instead of accepting the truth that he was where he wanted to be, and he was who he wanted to be with. I got mad and promised to leave him, but the minute I saw him, my heart settled, and my mind shifted to forgiveness mode until the next time. This cycle went on for years.

Being in this place was very miserable. I wasted a lot of years trying to love what I never had. Trying to hold on to what held on to me because of what I could do for it. I clearly read in the Bible that when a man finds a wife, he finds a good thing and obtains favor from the Lord (Proverbs 18:22). How bout my mind convinced me that my job is to help, love, forgive, and go through with a man and he would love me in return. My mistake was doing wife things with my boyfriend, soul mate, significant other, Boo, Bae, etc). When this didn't work, I found myself on the roller coaster again.

Your issue may not be a man or woman. It can be anything. Anything that has a strong hold on you or anything that causes your mind stress. It could be indecisiveness, money, drugs, people, places, sex, low self-esteem, work, lack of work, trauma, stress, feeling like nothing is working in your life, drama, rejection, hurt, pain, depression, anxiety, guilt, fear, anger, feelings of failure, hopelessness, not being able to say "no", lending, and/or settling. When things consume us, We find ourselves in a place where we may feel like things are BROKE and cannot be fixed. After all, you have tried everything possible to fix it, but you find yourself anxious, worrying, and/or stressing about "it". If you are honest, a lot of the "its" are things that you cannot control.

If you have walked in any of the shoes above, this journey is for you. For those like I was (in denial), this journey is definitely for you. You see, I could see stuff in others, but failed to see me. I had my hands in everything around me. I volunteered for things and overextended myself trying to fix "it". When "it" was ME! I lied to myself daily. I was miserable but pretending to be OKAY. I created a perfect world in my mind. I knew how to fix others, but I couldn't see "Me". Seeing me was one of the hardest thing I ever had to do. My mind convinced me that it was everyone else. I was everything to everybody, but nothing to myself. I was taught to give, but didn't know how to give to self.

I gave out a long time ago. I ran off everyone else's fuel when mine was gone. When those people "left", I was stranded in the middle of the road with no gas. I couldn't go forward, I couldn't go backwards. I couldn't even pull off the road. It was like my mind shut down and I didn't know what to do. I didn't know which way to turn. SAY But God! I was stuck. My mind began to replay events that led to this place, but it didn't get far because the world that I created in my mind was crumbling down around me. Because my life was built on everyone else, when they changed and/or shifted, my life changed and shifted also. I had to find clarity and get focused.

We need to R.E.S.P.O.N.D. and not react in every situation. If you didn't know "it", let me share with you that trials will come (2 Corinthians 4:8-9 NIV-says **8** We are hard pressed on every side, but not crushed; perplexed, but not in despair; **9** persecuted, but not abandoned; struck down, but not destroyed). You have tried so many things to help fix the "it's" in your life (drugs, sex, marriage, work, traveling, being the other man or woman, loving others more than you love "self", taking care of others when you are empty etc.). SAY But God! I ask that you Turn to God and His words during times of adversity for strength and comfort. When we put our faith in him, he will help guide us to the path of happiness and peace. I also accept the fact that I created the path that I got stuck on. I allowed, settled, and accepted things that was toxic in my life.

I ask that you take this 7 day journey intended to help you refocus on your life and purpose. This journey may not make sense. You may not be able to figure it out before hand, but know that "it" will work out for your good. This journey will not cure every situation and issue that you have, but it will take you to the GREATER. A place where your mind can be free from **brokenness,** worry, stress, anxiety, depression, and instability. 1 Peter 5:10 NLT tells me that In his kindness God called you to share in his eternal glory by means of Christ Jesus. So after you have suffered a little while, he will restore, support, and strengthen you, and he will place you on a firm foundation. Decide today that you have suffered enough! That situation that you are in is not permanent. It may seem impossible to get out of and/or overcome, but God is faithful and he will help you in your time of need.

Over the next 7 days, I ask you to commit to the process. Each day, you will find a key to focus on mending your broken mind, a daily scripture to meditate on daily, insightful words and examples to help clear your mind, and a prayer. Each day, set aside a time and place free of distractions and read the daily encouragement. There is a journal entry on the back of each page to jot down your thoughts, words of comfort, healing, and/or notes. Repeat this journey as many times as you need to until you are restored, strengthened, and love yourself.

YOU were created with purpose. GOD had a plan for you even before you were born. Jeremiah 29:11 (NIV) says [11] For I know the plans I have for you," declares the LORD, "plans to prosper you and not to harm you, plans to give you hope and a future. **What is your hope in? Trust the process and change your future.**

DAY ONE

RENEW MY MIND?
Scripture for today: Romans 12: 2 (NIV)

[2] Do not conform to the pattern of this world, but be transformed by the renewing of your mind. Then you will be able to test and approve what God's will is—his good, pleasing and perfect will.

Each day I urge you to respect you body. If you are single, sex outside of marriage is a sin. If I'm not married to a person, then I shouldn't be having sex no matter what he/she tells me. If that person loved and respected you; they wouldn't be pressuring you into having sex and/or vice versa. If you are legally married, sex with anyone other than your spouse is a sin. In other words, common law, someone you are dating, your secret, your cut man or woman, your girlfriend, boyfriend, significant other, engaged to, Boo, Bae, Sugar, Sweetie, Baby etc- IT IS STILL A SIN UNTIL YOU GET MARRIED. That's why it's important to keep our mind clear and pure. We cannot do things the way the world does them. We MUST do it God's way. At times, we cannot control what thoughts enter our minds, but we can take control of these thoughts through God's word. His word helps us recognize the thought(s), teach us how to respond to these thoughts, and help us rebuke any ungodly thoughts that enter our mind. What you magnify will manifest. If you think on (meditate) on something long enough, it most likely will come to pass. We must not allow our minds to wonder out of control. We must renew it by reading what God says we should do in certain situations. It's easy to go along with traditions, habits, and/or beliefs, but our beliefs must line up with the word of God in order to calm and renew our minds.

Do a Bible Topic search on: Scriptures on Renewing My Mind, medicate on them, and jot down your thoughts.

Prayer for today:

Lord, as I pray today, help me to open my mind so that it can be renewed. Help me to see things as you see them. Help me to take time to study and meditate on your scriptures so that my mind can be renewed. Thank You Lord for a renewed mind. In Jesus Name, Amen.

NOTES FOR TODAY

DAY TWO

EXAMINE YOURSELF?

Scripture for today: 2 Corinthians 13:5
Test Yourselves to see if you are in the faith; examine yourselves! Or do you not recognize this about yourselves, that Jesus Christ is in you—unless indeed you fail the test?

It's so easy to examine others. It's easy to point out their flaws and shortcomings. Today meditate and ask God to Tell You about you (Show You your rebellion and sin). When God begin to show you, other people may pop in your mind but remember when you see their rebellion, sin, and shortcomings, these are your character flaws, defect, sin, and rebellion that God is showing you through others. It's time to do a heart and mind check. When magnified, simply repent and begin to work on these things. What are you thinking about most? What do you spend most of your time doing? What issues do you have that need to change? What habits do you need to adjust? What are you speaking? What are you looking at? What are you listening to? Who are you listening to?

Do a Bible Topic search on: Scriptures on Evaluating/Examining Yourself and jot a few of them down.

Prayer for today:

Lord, as I come to you today, I come with an open mind and heart. Help me to examine myself and focus on me today and not on others around me. Help me to see my rebellion and sin and show me what I need to change about me. Help me to work on these things Lord. In Jesus Name, Amen.

NOTES FOR TODAY

DAY THREE

SPEND TIME WITH GOD?

Scripture for today: Psalm 16:11 (AMP)

[11] You will show me the path of life; In Your presence is fullness of joy; In Your right hand there are pleasures forevermore.

This verse changed my life. It helped me get it settled in my mind, heart, soul, and spirit, that God would show me the path of life and in his Presence is fullness of joy. But more so, in his righthand there are pleasures forevermore. I realized that the pleasures that I sought from people, places, and things were temporary. True joy and happiness came from Christ and the AWESOME part is that God is not an petty. He won't give it to me and then take his joy away from me. I can choose the wrong path in life and experience many sorrows, heartache, and sadness looking for pleasures that are temporary. However, if I trust God to show me the path that he has set for me and I travel that road, He is there with me and being in his presence is fullness of joy. And those pleasures that I seek, I can trust God to give me pleasures forevermore. **Say, Lord, I trust you to show me the path of life that you have chose for me. Help me to stay in your presence because there is fullness of joy there, and help me trust that the pleasures that you give me are forevermore and not temporary.** God wants quality time. We don't have to believe the lies of the enemy. He comes to kill steal and destroy, but God came that you may have an abundant life. Why are you giving the enemy space in your mind? Spending time with God will help us grow spiritually and develop the gifts he put inside of us. The only way to experience the abundant life is to know Him for yourself.

Do a Bible Topic search on scriptures on Spending time with God.

Prayer for Today:

Lord today, help me spend time with you today. Help me not be so busy that I cannot hear from you today. As I spend time with you, show me what I need to do in order to make time to spend with you daily. My desire is to spend time with you daily. In Jesus Name, Amen.

NOTES FOR TODAY

DAY FOUR

What If...

PRAY ABOUT WHO You LET IN Your Life?
Scripture for today: Philippians 4:6-7

Do not be anxious about anything, but in every situation, by prayer and petition, with thanksgiving, present your requests to God. And the peace of God, which transcends all understanding, will guard your hearts and your minds in Christ Jesus.

We need to pray about everything that we face. Not just in times of distress or need, but we should talk to God daily through prayer as we move through our day. We don't have to be anxious about who is or who is not in our lives. We don't have to settle. It's about God's timing and trusting him to bring it to pass. If we want a mate, pray about it and allow God to show you what to do. I remember when I wanted a husband, I got very anxious about every man I saw wondering is he my husband. One day while praying, I read that if I don't get anxious, but in every situation pray and petition God with thanksgiving that His peace which surpasses all understanding will guard (calm) my heart and mind in Jesus Christ. I found out that there were times when I felt rejected, but during these difficult times, Man's rejection was God's protecting me from what was to come. You see, I only know what someone tell me about themselves, but God knows all (all their secrets, hurts, pains, good, not so good, sin, ways, character, heart, and mind). So I need to seek him about who I let in my life. He will show me if I let him and I need to believe him the 1st time. Pray and meditate on any anxieties that you may have about what you don't have and thank God for giving you what you need and not what you thought you needed. God is faithful, he keeps good records, and prayer works. Pray his word.

Do a Bible Topic search on scriptures on prayer and/or praying.

Prayer for Today:
Lord Jesus, help me to pray your word. Help me to pray to pray the solution to my problems instead of the problem. Help me to pray about everything and with thanksgiving in my heart. Thank you for protecting me when I felt rejected. In Jesus Name, Amen.

NOTES FOR TODAY

DAY FIVE

OBEY THE WORD

Scripture for today: Proverbs 3:5-6

(5) Trust in the LORD with all thine heart; and lean not unto thine own understanding. [6] In all thy ways acknowledge him, and he shall direct thy paths.

If you obey God's word, you will be blessed. I may not understand it. It may not make sense. I may not be able to figure it out, but I will trust God and obey his word. God word is full of wisdom for our daily lives. I obey his word because of His love for me (He gave his only begotten Son that I may have life and not perish). Obeying God's word, helps us get along with each other. We must obey God's word and live according to it, BUT in order to obey God's word, I MUST KNOW IT. How do I learn God's word? We must be diligent and read God's word daily to strengthen our faith and renew our mind. If you are struggling in a specific area that need change and/or growth, do a topic search and dig deeper into the word of God to find out what God says about that topic. The apply and submit yourself to God's word. Everything you need is in the word of God. Every situation that you will ever face; God has an answer for it in His word. Try it and see. Luke 11:28 (KJV) says [28] But he said, Yea rather, blessed are they that hear the word of God, and keep it. Read his word daily. Meditate on it. Ask God what it means if you are unsure. Study God's word and apply it to your life immediately.

Do a Bible Topic search on scriptures on obeying God's word.

Prayer for Today:

Lord Jesus help me obey your word. Help me to diligently study your word and obey it. Lord, I am struggling with_____ help me find scriptures on this topic, apply it and submit to it. Help me to obey your word in every area of my life. In Jesus Name, Amen.

NOTES FOR TODAY

DAY SIX

NEVER FORGET WHAT GOD SAYS LOVE IS

Scripture for today: 1 Corinthians 13:4-7 (NIV) [4] Love is patient, love is kind. It does not envy, it does not boast, it is not proud. [5] It does not dishonor others, it is not self-seeking, it is not easily angered, it keeps no record of wrongs. [6] Love does not delight in evil but rejoices with the truth. [7] It always protects, always trusts, always hopes, always perseveres.

It's easy to associate love with a "feeling". At times, we think we can fall in and out of love with someone. I hear people say, "I love you", but "I'm not in love with you". Well according to God's word, you cannot separate love. It's patient, kind, does not envy, does not boast, it not proud, doesn't dishonor others, is not self-seeking, not easily angered, keeps no record of wrongs, does not delight in evil, rejoices with truth, always protects, always trusts, always hopes, and always perseveres. I used to make excuses and think that no one could ever love like this. So I ignored a lot of the above requirements that God left showing me how to love myself and others. After learning and obeying God's word, I realized that if God commanded me to do it; he equipped me with what I need to bring it to pass. I pray daily that I love like Christ said love. When I focused on was I loving like this and not so much on was others loving like this; it helped me to love according to God's word. My desire is to reach a place where I can love like Jesus. Jesus said in **John 15:12-13** "This is My commandment, that you love one another, just as I have loved you". In order to help me in this area, I pray Psalm 53:10-11 daily: 10Create in me a clean heart, O God, And renew a steadfast spirit within me. 11Do not cast me away from Your presence And do not take Your Holy Spirit from me....**Check your heart today and see are you loving like God says we should.**

Do a Bible Topic search on scriptures on What God says love is.

PRAYER FOR TODAY:
Lord Jesus, help me to love like you say to love. I thank you for loving me even when I wasn't so lovable. Lord, help me to love others and help myself so that I will know my self-worth. Lord create in me a clean heart and renew a steadfast spirit within me. I thank you. In Jesus Name, Amen.

NOTES FOR TODAY

DAY SEVEN

DEALT WITH YOUR ISSUES?

Scripture for today: Romans 8:28

And we know that all things work together for good to them that love God, to them who are the called according to *his* purpose.

Satan is on a mission: to kill, steal, and to destroy us. He is very deceitful and entices us making us believe we need certain things mainly focusing on what we don't have. He tries to steal our joy, kill our spirit, and destroy us. Satan tempted Jesus (Mathew 4:1-11), but he resisted him. The word tells us what he is trying to do in 1 Peter 5:8-9-8 (i.e. KJV ®)**Be sober-minded and alert. Your adversary the devil prowls around like a roaring lion, seeking someone to devour.** 9 Resist him, standing firm in your faith and in the knowledge that your brothers throughout the world are undergoing the same kinds of suffering. Don't give him power over you. If his job is to kill, steal, and destroy, why in the world are you still running and hanging with him? Would you drink poison if you knew what it was and what it would do to you? Don't be held hostage to your current or past issues, sins, shame, or guilt, habits, addictions. God will take all of your pain and turn it into purpose. He will take the mess and turn it into a message. He cares for you. It will all work out for your good. 1 Peter 5:8-9 -7Cast all your anxiety on Him, because He cares for you. It's time to **R.E.S.P.O.N.D. R**enew Your Mind, **E**valuate/examine self, **S**pend time with God, **P**ray, **O**bey The word, **N**ever Forget what God says about love, and **D**eal with your issues. Do not react to things that we cannot control and/or that are not pleasing to God. Cast your cares on Him.

Do a Bible Topic search on scriptures on Dealing with your issues.

PRAYER FOR TODAY:

Lord, I don't understand how things will work out, but I trust you. I can't see my way, but you will make a way for me. You created me from nothing, so Lord I know you can recreate me. Cast out anything that should not be in me. Give me the strength to move forward on the path you've laid out for me.

NOTES FOR TODAY

CONCLUSION

Finally, when mending BROKENESS, we must SET "IT"! (DECIDE to change our current circumstances), LET 'IT' GO! (If it leaves; God has something better for you) LEAVE "IT" ALONE (Trust the Process) AND LET "IT" HEAL (We cannot hasten how others heal and/or move forward). Our focus must be on allowing time for self to heal when it has experienced things. We can't jump from relationship to relationship without taking time to heal. We can't jump from job to job without reflecting on our contribution to our stress. We can't love others where we don't even love ourselves. The body was created to heal itself and we have but one body. Stop trying to fix "IT" (things you CANNOT control) and focus on being the "You" that God created you to be.

Ask Yourself These Questions? What were you created to do? What dreams do you have about your future that you have abandoned? Who are you listening to? Do you care for yourself? What has God told you to do with your life? What reoccurring idea(s) or thoughts do you have that won't go away? What you do spend most of your time thinking about? Pray on these things and allow God to direct your paths. He said in Proverbs 3:5-6 [5] Trust in the LORD with all thine heart; and lean not unto thine own understanding. [6] In all thy ways acknowledge him, and he shall direct thy paths.

Brokenness attracts brokenness. Wholeness will discern brokenness. Remember, No matter what you do for someone else, if they want to leave you; they will. There is no amount of money, gifts, service, time, or anything else that can make them stay unless it's in there heart. Stop trying to do so much and just be what you were created to be. God will add to our lives in due season if we allow him to. Matthew 6:33 (KJV) tells us to [33] But seek ye first the kingdom of God, and his righteousness; and all these things shall be added unto you. Trust me; God will give you the desires of your heart if you serve him and those desires line up with His word. Please know that God won't ever give you another's person's husband or wife, so if you are with someone else's husband/wife that is not of God and it won't work. If you desire to be married, work on being the best spouse to the husband/wife that God has prepared and/or is preparing for you. Study God's word on being a wife/husband and submit to it. Stop worrying about what you don't have and wait on God.

Take time every day to rest and relax your mind. Think about positive things. If you are surrounded by negative things/situations, R.E.S.P.O.N.D. to them so that your mind will be clear. A clear mind increases our ability to think clearly so that we can make wise decisions without distortion, deception, and/or irrational beliefs. Unlearning what we have learned takes time. We must take the first step so that that we are clear minded and an enjoy life. Even if it means loving me until I am okay with being me, being with me, and being my best friend. It takes FAITH to love like this, but God is faithful and He promised me that he would NEVER leave nor forsake me.

I hope this journey helped clear your mind. In all of the searching and settling, I came to know that a clear mind is a "mended" mind. When I have mind issues; usually there are heart issues. As a man thinketh so is he. How do I know when my mind is mended? When I am able to do what it says in Philippians 4:8 (NLT) [8] And now, dear brothers and sisters, one final thing. Fix your thoughts on what is true, and honorable, and right, and pure, and lovely, and admirable. Think about things that are excellent and worthy of praise. Know your worth!

I have one last question for you?

Based on your current situation, if you died right now, where would you spend eternity? There's only two final resting places: Heaven or Hell. A lot of people struggle with where they will spend eternity. There is a way to know that you know that you know that you can spend eternity in Heaven. Romans 10:9-10 (KJV) says [9] That if thou shalt confess with thy mouth the Lord Jesus, and shalt believe in thine heart that God hath raised him from the dead, thou shalt be saved. [10] For with the heart man believeth unto righteousness; and with the mouth confession is made unto salvation.

PRAYER OF SALVATION

If you are unsure and want to be sure, pray this prayer: **Lord Jesus, I confess with my mouth and believe in my heart that God raised you from the dead. I ask you to forgive me of my sins. Come into my heart and be my Lord and Saviour. I thank you for saving me. In Jesus Name, Amen.**

If you said this prayer and accepted Jesus as your Lord and Saviour, please jot down the date below.

Date: _____

Made in the USA
Columbia, SC
26 September 2023

23250806R10017